ANIMALS of the USA
ACTIVITY BOOK

CLAIRE SAUNDERS

ILLUSTRATED BY BETHANY LORD

Kane Miller
A DIVISION OF EDC PUBLISHING

CONTENTS

4 WELCOME TO THE **ANIMALS OF THE USA** ACTIVITY BOOK

6 BEFORE YOU GET STARTED...

- **8** All-American Animals
- **9** National Park Scramble
- **10** Climb the Mountain
- **11** Name that Crowd
- **12** Balance the Bison
- **13** Desert I-Spy
- **14** Where's My Mom?
- **15** Animalville, USA
- **16** Follow the Flyway
- **17** Salamander Species
- **18** Take the Trail
- **19** Quiz Time!
- **20** All at Sea
- **21** Backyard Bandit
- **22** Prairie Dog Maze
- **23** Design a Quarter
- **24** Presidential Pets
- **25** Hibernation Crisscross
- **26** Odd Bird Out
- **27** Spider Search
- **28** What's Odd in Alaska?
- **29** Give Me a Job!
- **30** The Great Armadillo Count
- **31** Tide Pool Tale
- **32** Snake Color by Numbers
- **33** Metamorphosis Maze

34	Far-Out Festivals	47	Hold the Front Page!
35	Count the Catch	48	Split the Wolf Packs
36	Only in America	49	Draw a Hummingbird
37	Minibeast Sudoku	50	True or False?
38	Under the Sea	51	Hawaii Word Search
39	Turtle Time	52	Deer States
40	Crack the Codes	53	Monarch of the Skies
41	Hide-and-Seek	54	Who, What, Where?
42	Nickname that State	55	Find the Fish
43	Study the Scene	56	Copy the Mammoth
44	Everglades Word Hunt	57	You Choose
45	Deadly Critter Crossword		
46	Ranch Roundup	58	Answers

Welcome to the ANIMALS OF THE USA ACTIVITY BOOK

From tiny hummingbirds to enormous humpback whales, the United States is home to an amazing array of animals. As you color and puzzle your way through this activity book, you'll discover lots of fascinating facts about the creatures, great and small, that make the US so special.

First, read the fun facts on these pages, then grab your pens and pencils and dive into the activities!

If you get stuck, the answers are at the back of the book.

In Talkeetna, Alaska, a cat called Stubbs was the mayor for 20 years!

Hawaii's state fish is the Humuhumunukunukuāpua'a. It's pronounced "who-moo-who-moo-noo-koo-noo-koo-ah-poo-ah-ah."

The Gila monster is a venomous lizard that can grow up to 2 feet long! It lives in the deserts of the southwestern US.

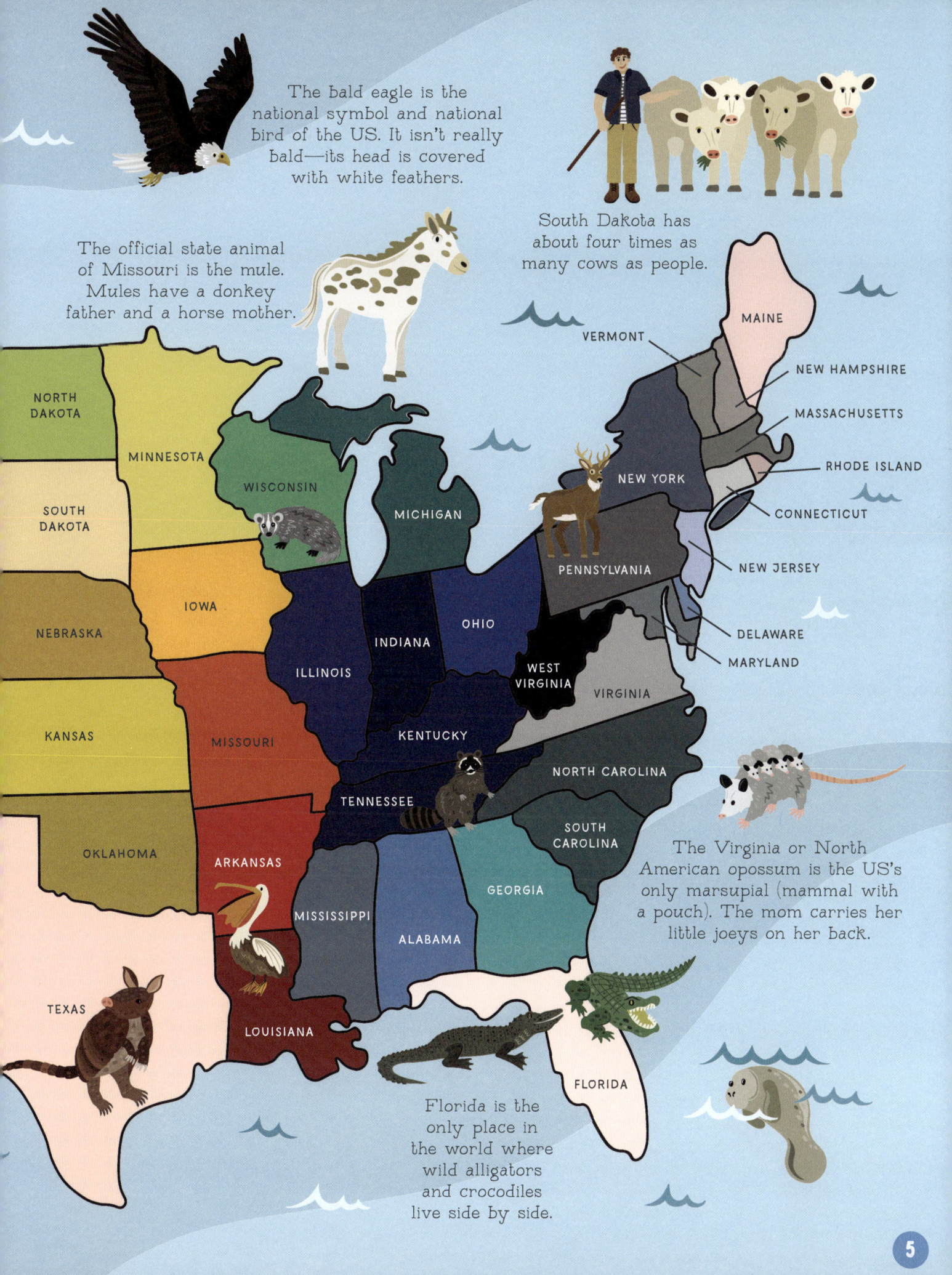

BEFORE you get STARTED...

This page shows just some of the amazing animals included in this book. Check the boxes of all the animals you would like to see in real life. If you have been lucky enough to see any of the animals already, color in the check boxes.

MOOSE ☐

DOLPHIN ☐

PRAIRIE DOG ☐

MONARCH BUTTERFLY ☐

WOLVERINE ☐

GRAY WOLF ☐

HUMMINGBIRD ☐

ALLIGATOR ☐

BLACK BEAR ☐

AMERICAN GOLDFINCH ☐

RACCOON ☐

ARMADILLO ☐

COYOTE ☐

JACKRABBIT ☐

Write the name of your favorite animal here. It can be one of the animals above, or a different animal.

_____

WHERE AM I?

As you go through the puzzles in this book, look for the five animals pictured below. Once you find them, fill in the name of the state that they live in.

TUFTED PUFFIN
STATE:_____

DEVILS HOLE PUPFISH
STATE:_____

ISLAND FOX
STATE:_____

NENE
STATE:_____

DALL SHEEP
STATE:_____

7

ALL-AMERICAN ANIMALS

The United States is home to all kinds of creatures. Most of the animals on this page live in the wild in the US, but three of them don't! Can you spot and circle the imposters?

- BALD EAGLE 
- COYOTE  
- HIPPO
- WHITE-TAILED DEER  
- MOUNTAIN LION 
- BEAVER 
- MEERKAT 
- GIANT PANDA
- NORTHERN ELEPHANT SEAL  
- ELK

NATIONAL PARK SCRAMBLE

Have you ever visited a national park? Sixty-three national parks protect some of the US's most spectacular landscapes, and the animals that live in them.

Unscramble the letters below each national park sign to reveal a well-known animal that can be found there.

OOMES

_ _ _ _ _

NSIBO

_ _ _ _ _

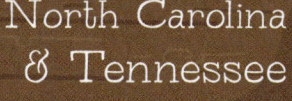

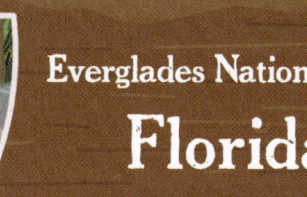

KBALC REAB

_ _ _ _ _   _ _ _ _

LGATRLIOA

_ _ _ _ _ _ _ _ _

NAME THAT CROWD

YOU'VE PROBABLY HEARD OF A PACK OF WOLVES OR A HERD OF CATTLE, BUT HOW ABOUT A SHIVER OF SHARKS OR A PRICKLE OF PORCUPINES? SOMETIMES, THE GROUP NAME FOR AN ANIMAL DESCRIBES THEM PERFECTLY! CAN YOU USE YOUR IMAGINATION TO THINK UP NEW GROUP NAMES FOR THESE COMMON AMERICAN ANIMALS?

A ~~herd~~ _____ of bison

A ~~pack~~ _____ of coyotes

COYOTES LIVE IN SMALL FAMILY GROUPS MADE UP OF A MOM, A DAD, AND THEIR PUPS.

A ~~colony~~ _____ of beavers

A ~~nest~~ _____ of snakes

LOUISIANA IS THE STATE WITH THE MOST ALLIGATORS—THERE ARE ALMOST 2 MILLION OF THEM!

A ~~congregation~~ _____ of alligators

IN THE WINTER, SOME SNAKES SNUGGLE TOGETHER TO STAY WARM!

WHERE'S MY MOM?

THE ANIMALS BELOW ARE ALL MAMMALS THAT CAN BE FOUND IN THE UNITED STATES. THEY EACH GIVE BIRTH TO THEIR YOUNG, AND THE MOMS FEED AND PROTECT THE BABIES UNTIL THEY ARE READY TO LOOK AFTER THEMSELVES.

Here's an example:

Draw lines to connect the babies to their moms.

The lines can go up and down, left and right, but not diagonally, and the lines must not cross.

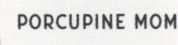

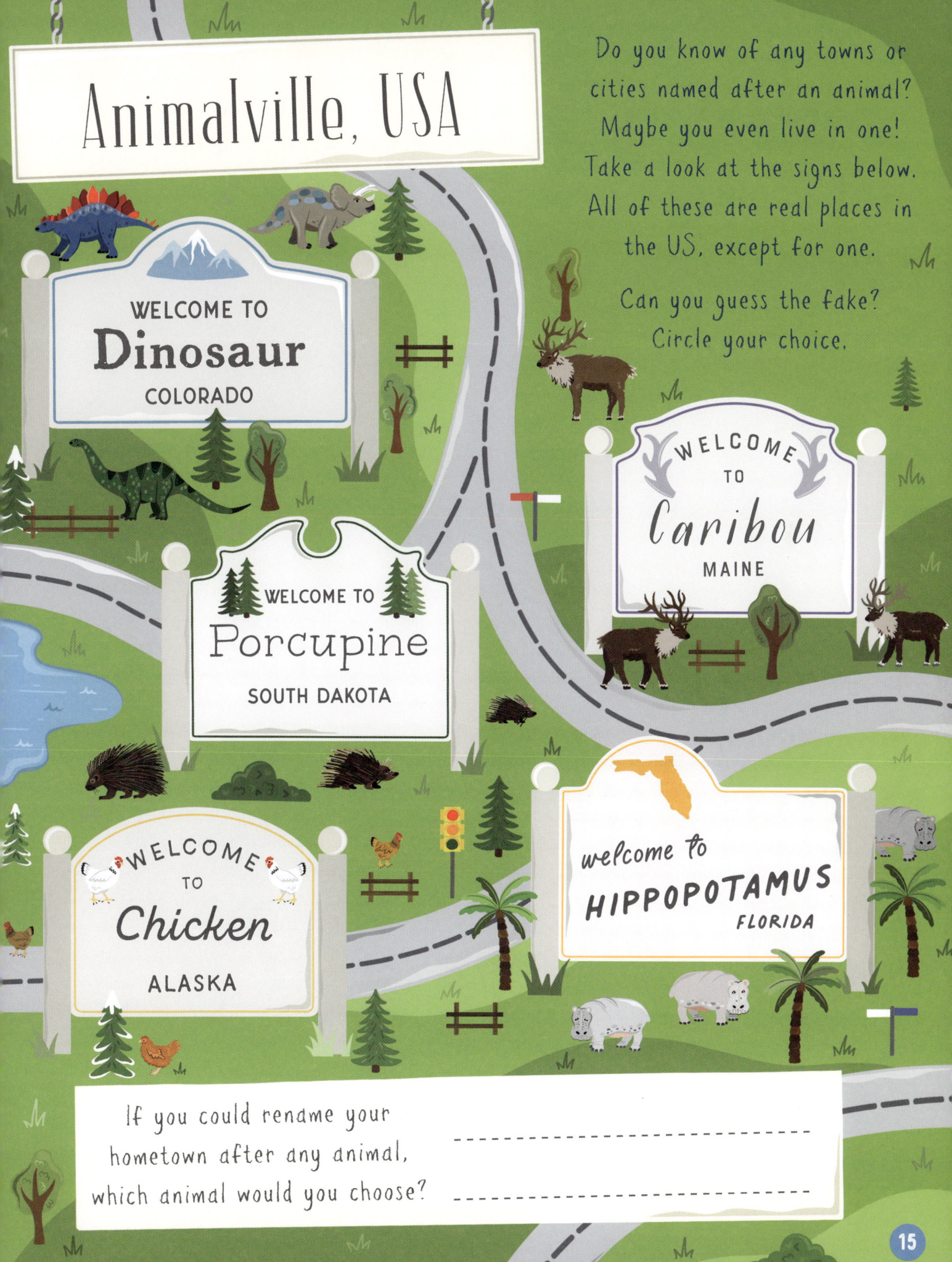

TAKE THE TRAIL

Yellowstone National Park in Wyoming, Montana, and Idaho is one of the best places in the US to spot big animals such as bison, elk, moose, and bears.

Follow the directions below to take a tour around the park. Which three animals do you pass on your route? Circle each one.

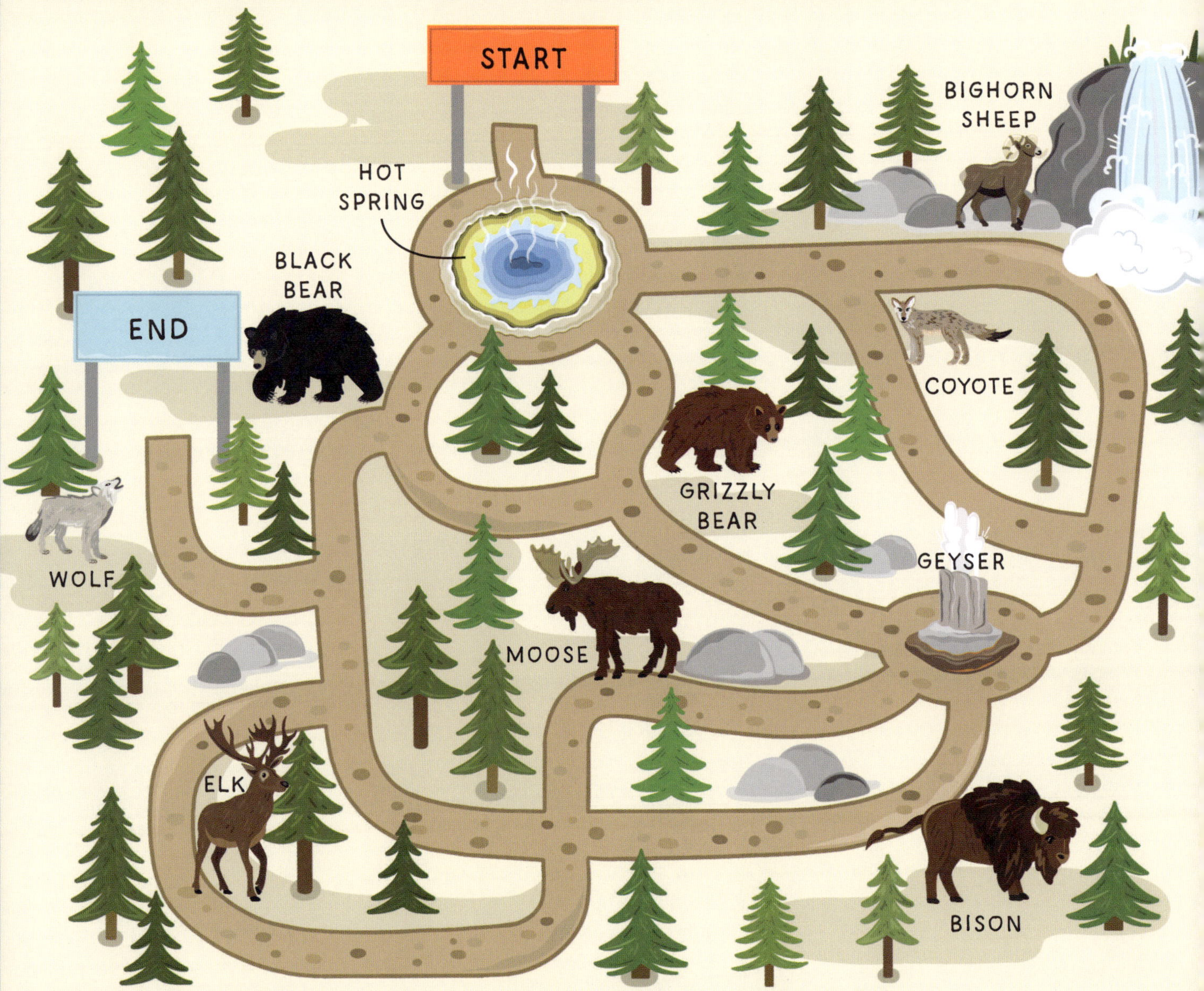

DIRECTIONS

1. Head east at the hot spring.

2. When you arrive at a fork in the path, take the path on the right.

3. At the next fork in the path, head south.

4. At the geyser, take the path heading south.

5. When you reach the crossroads, choose the path that leads west.

6. Continue on the path until you pass three boulders, then make a turn west.

Quiz Time!

Time to test your animal knowledge! Can you figure out the answers to these multiple-choice questions?

Check one answer box for each question.

1. The bite of which US animal is strong enough to crush a bowling ball?

- ☐ a) Mountain goat
- ☐ b) Grizzly bear
- ☐ c) Coyote

2. Which animal can jump at least 20 times the length of its own body?

- ☐ a) Pronghorn
- ☐ b) Dolphin
- ☐ c) Kangaroo rat

3. When a male porcupine sees a female he likes, what does he do?

- ☐ a) Pees on her
- ☐ b) Shakes his spines and stands on his head
- ☐ c) Runs away and hides

4. What can a North American horned lizard squirt 3 feet from its eye?

- ☐ a) Tears
- ☐ b) Blood
- ☐ c) Pee

ALL AT SEA

The US is home to all kinds of marine animals. If you head out to sea at Glacier Bay National Park in Alaska, you might spot humpback whales diving, sea otters bobbing on their backs, or tufted puffins skimming the waves.

Draw two straight lines to split the picture below into three parts, so that each part has one whale, one otter, and one puffin. Each line should run from one edge of the picture to another, and the lines must not cross.

Here's an example:

Puffins can carry lots of fish in their beak at once—the record is 62!

Humpback whales eat about 5,000 pounds of krill, plankton, and fish every day.

Groups of sea otters sleep holding paws, so that they don't drift away from each other.

BACKYARD BANDIT

Has a raccoon ever visited your backyard? These furry-faced mammals are found all over the United States, and are known as scavengers that raid vegetable gardens and garbage cans. They can even open latches and locks!

This pesky raccoon has upturned a trash can with eight items inside. Study the picture for 1 minute, then cover it with a piece of paper, and write down as many of the items as you can remember.

1. ....
2. ....
3. ....
4. ....
5. ....
6. ....
7. ....
8. ....

DESIGN A QUARTER

BIRDS, BUTTERFLIES, BEAVERS, AND BISON ARE JUST SOME OF THE ANIMALS THAT HAVE BEEN ENGRAVED ONTO UNITED STATES COINS. IF YOU COULD CHOOSE AN ANIMAL TO DECORATE A NEW COIN, WHICH ANIMAL WOULD IT BE?

DRAW YOUR DESIGN HERE:

UNITED STATES OF AMERICA

QUARTER DOLLAR

HERE ARE SOME IDEAS ...
- DRAW YOUR STATE'S OFFICIAL MAMMAL OR BIRD.
- CHOOSE YOUR FAVORITE ANIMAL IN THIS BOOK TO DRAW.
- DRAW YOUR PET, IF YOU HAVE ONE.
- DRAW THE NEXT ANIMAL YOU SEE, WHATEVER IT IS!

Presidential Pets

DID YOU KNOW THAT MOST US PRESIDENTS HAVE HAD PETS IN THE WHITE HOUSE? THERE HAVE BEEN DOGS, CATS, GUINEA PIGS, HORSES, A LIZARD, POSSUMS, AND EVEN A ONE-LEGGED ROOSTER!

IF YOU WERE THE PRESIDENT, WHAT PET WOULD YOU PICK? DRAW ITS PORTRAIT AND GIVE IT A NAME.

Hibernation Crisscross

WHEN WINTER ARRIVES AND TEMPERATURES DROP, SOME ANIMALS CURL UP IN A DARK, QUIET PLACE AND STAY THERE UNTIL SPRING. THE DEEP SLEEP THEY GO INTO, CALLED HIBERNATION, HELPS THEM TO SURVIVE THE WINTER.

FILL IN THE CRISSCROSS GRID, USING THE WORDS BELOW. EACH ONE IS THE NAME OF A HIBERNATING ANIMAL FOUND IN THE US.

9 LETTERS
bumblebee
groundhog

8 LETTERS
chipmunk
wood frog

7 LETTERS
ladybug

6 LETTERS
marmot

5 LETTERS
snail

4 LETTERS
bear

3 LETTERS
bat

ODD BIRD OUT

Did you know that every state has an official bird? Some states even share the same bird. Take a look at the state birds below. In each row, circle the bird that is different from the rest.

Cactus wrens sometimes build their nests in spiky cacti.

CACTUS WREN: Arizona

AMERICAN GOLDFINCH: New Jersey, Iowa, Washington

In winter, goldfinches burrow into the snow to keep warm.

Mockingbirds can mimic other birds, insects, and even car alarms!

MOCKINGBIRD: Arkansas, Florida, Texas, Tennessee, Mississippi

MOUNTAIN BLUEBIRD: Idaho, Nevada

Only the male bluebird is bright blue. The female is mainly gray.

Robins are one of the first birds to lay their eggs in spring.

AMERICAN ROBIN: Connecticut, Michigan, Wisconsin

Spider Search

There are about 3,500 different types of spider in the US. Most of them are harmless, but not all! Follow the instructions to uncover the name of the country's most venomous spider.

1. Look at the list of words below. Sometimes the color of a word matches the word (for example, RED), and sometimes it doesn't (for example, RED). Find and write the word that matches its color the most number of times. This is the first word of your deadly spider's name.

BLUE RED YELLOW WHITE BLACK
YELLOW GREEN RED WHITE GREEN BLUE
BLACK RED WHITE YELLOW BLUE GREEN
GREEN BLUE YELLOW BLUE GREEN RED
WHITE BLACK YELLOW BLUE BLACK RED

..............BLACK..............

2. To find the second word of your spider's name, cross out all of the green, blue, yellow, and white letters, and read the letters that remain. Write the word you find below.

KSDJWIAIEHFDMZIUOZGCVOOOAWHBV

..............WIDOW..............

What's Odd in Alaska?

Denali National Park in Alaska is a huge wilderness of dense forests, snow-cloaked mountains, and cold, treeless plains called tundra. Tourists come to the park hoping to spot "The Big Five": moose, caribou, grizzly bears, wolves, and curly-horned Dall sheep.

Take a look at the picture of Denali below and circle the six odd things that don't belong.

Give Me a Job!

Take a look at the animal-related job ads. Which would you most like to do? Pick your favorite, then write why you think you'd be great for the job.

ZOOKEEPER'S ASSISTANT
Duties include bottle-feeding the zoo babies, and chopping up fruit for the bears.

FILMMAKER'S ASSISTANT
Join our team in the Channel Islands National Park, California. We are making a documentary about the island fox, which is found nowhere else on Earth!

PET SITTER
Helper needed to look after three cats and take a puppy for walks.

ANIMAL RESCUE SANCTUARY VOLUNTEER
Come and help us look after injured and orphaned animals and release them back into the wild.

Hello,
I would like the job of _____

because _____

TIDE POOL TALE

ALONG THE ROCKY SHORELINE OF OLYMPIC NATIONAL PARK, WASHINGTON, MAGICAL TIDE POOLS APPEAR DURING LOW TIDE. THESE MINIATURE WORLDS ARE HOME TO EVERYTHING FROM TINY SEA SNAILS AND SCURRYING CRABS, TO COLORFUL SEA STARS AND ANEMONES.

IMAGINE YOU'RE LOOKING INTO ONE OF THESE TIDE POOLS. WHAT DO YOU FIND? WRITE A STORY ABOUT YOUR DISCOVERY.

METAMORPHOSIS MAZE

Like all amphibians, the North American wood frog goes through some big changes as it grows up. In a process called "metamorphosis," it starts out as an egg, and then turns into a tadpole, before eventually becoming an adult frog.

To find a path through the maze below, you must move from square to square following the same sequence:

Egg – Tadpole – Frog

You can move up, down, left, or right, but you cannot move diagonally.

START

END

The wood frog has a neat trick to survive the winter—it freezes itself! When the weather warms up again, the frog's blood thaws and its heart restarts.

FAR-OUT FESTIVALS

Check out these weird and wonderful animal-themed festivals. Three of them are real, and two are made up. Can you spot which?

Circle the two fakes.

Hank's Hound Hoedown

Bring your pooch along to America's biggest dog dancing extravaganza.

Hop Springs, New Jersey

Woolly Worm Festival

WATCH TWO WORMS RACE UP A PIECE OF STRING.

BANNER ELK, NORTH CAROLINA

CROC JUMP FESTIVAL

LEAP OVER LIVE CROCODILES. (GROWN-UPS ONLY!)

SNAPS HUT CREEK, DELAWARE

WISCONSIN STATE COW CHIP THROW

TOSS DRIED COW DUNG AS FAR AS YOU CAN—NO GLOVES ALLOWED!

PRAIRIE DU SAC, WISCONSIN

Wayne Chicken Show

Join in the world's largest chicken dance.

Wayne, Nebraska

If you could make up your own wacky animal festival, what would it be called, and what would it be famous for?

_____

_____

_____

only in AMERICA

The tiny critters on this page are so rare they are each only found in one particular place in the US, and nowhere else in the world!

MISSISSIPPI GOPHER FROG

LOCATION: Three ponds in southern Mississippi

DEVILS HOLE PUPFISH

LOCATION: One pool in Death Valley, Nevada

YOSEMITE CAVE PSEUDOSCORPION

LOCATION: Two caves in Yosemite National Park, California

Imagine you have discovered a completely new species in a pond near your home. What does it look like? Draw it below, and name your discovery.

Name: ....

NEW SPECIES ARE DISCOVERED ALL THE TIME. SCIENTISTS THINK THERE ARE MILLIONS OF SPECIES STILL WAITING TO BE FOUND!

MINIBEAST SUDOKU

Billions of bugs can be found crawling and scuttling around the US—out in the wilderness, in your backyard, even in your home!

Complete the sudoku puzzle by filling each square with a picture of a slug, spider, beetle, or ladybug. Each minibeast can appear only once in each row, column, and mini grid.

The silk of the golden silk orb weaver spider is eight times stronger than steel.

A ladybug might eat more than 5,000 insects in its lifetime.

Pinacate beetles live in the deserts of western North America. Some species scare off predators by standing on their head and spraying a stinky black liquid.

The bright-yellow banana slug thrives in the cool, damp forests of the Pacific Northwest.

UNDER THE SEA

YOU WOULD NEED A SNORKEL TO EXPLORE BISCAYNE NATIONAL PARK, IN FLORIDA, BECAUSE 95% OF IT IS UNDERWATER! IF YOU'RE LUCKY, YOU MIGHT SPOT MANATEES AND SEA TURTLES GLIDING PAST THE COLORFUL CORAL AND SWAYING SEAGRASS.

THERE ARE EIGHT DIFFERENCES BETWEEN THESE TWO PICTURES OF BISCAYNE. FIND AND CIRCLE THEM ALL.

CRACK THE CODES

WHICH AMERICAN ANIMAL IS THE FASTEST? BIGGEST? TALLEST? TO FIND OUT, YOU'LL NEED TO CRACK THE CODES BELOW. USE THE TABLES TO HELP YOU. FIRST, FIND THE CODED LETTER ON THE TOP ROW OF THE TABLE—THE LETTER BELOW IT IS THE ANSWER.

1. THE LETTERS IN THIS CODE HAVE BEEN SHIFTED ONE TO THE RIGHT. SO, FOR EXAMPLE, "A" BECOMES "B," "B" BECOMES "C," AND SO ON.

Z	A	B	C	D	E	F	G	H	I	J	K	L	M	N	O	P	Q	R	S	T	U	V	W	X	Y
A	B	C	D	E	F	G	H	I	J	K	L	M	N	O	P	Q	R	S	T	U	V	W	X	Y	Z

WHAT IS AMERICA'S FASTEST LAND ANIMAL?

O Q N M F G N Q M

2. THE LETTERS IN THIS CODE HAVE BEEN SHIFTED ONE TO THE LEFT. SO, FOR EXAMPLE, "B" BECOMES "A," AND SO ON.

B	C	D	E	F	G	H	I	J	K	L	M	N	O	P	Q	R	S	T	U	V	W	X	Y	Z	A
A	B	C	D	E	F	G	H	I	J	K	L	M	N	O	P	Q	R	S	T	U	V	W	X	Y	Z

WHAT IS AMERICA'S BIGGEST LAND ANIMAL?

C J T P O

3. EACH LETTER IN THIS CODE HAS BEEN SHIFTED EITHER ONE TO THE LEFT OR ONE TO THE RIGHT. SO, FOR EXAMPLE, A "B" COULD BE EITHER AN "A" OR A "C." THIS MEANS THERE ARE TWO POSSIBLE ANSWERS FOR EACH LETTER. TRICKY! USING THE TWO TABLES ABOVE, WRITE DOWN BOTH POSSIBLE ANSWERS FOR EACH LETTER. THEN SEE IF YOU CAN WORK OUT WHICH LETTERS ARE THE CORRECT ONES!

WHAT IS AMERICA'S TALLEST ANIMAL?

N   P   P   R   D
OR   OR   OR   OR   OR

Hide-and-Seek

The black-tailed jackrabbit (also called the American desert hare) is found in the western United States. Its big ears help it to keep cool.

Look carefully at this jumble of shapes. Can you find a jackrabbit hidden in among them? When you spot it, color it in!

NICKNAME THAT STATE

Did you know that many states have an animal-themed nickname? Use the clues below to help you work out which nickname belongs to which state. Draw lines to connect them.

BEAVER STATE

BADGER STATE

PELICAN STATE

WOLVERINE STATE

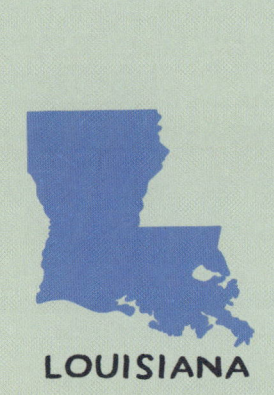
LOUISIANA

MICHIGAN

OREGON

WISCONSIN

CLUES:

- Michigan's animal does not begin with B.
- Louisiana's animal does not have fur.
- The animal for Oregon builds dams and lodges.
- The badger is the nickname for a state that has 9 letters.

STUDY THE SCENE

The beautiful Appalachian-Blue Ridge forests stretch from Pennsylvania in the north to Alabama in the south. Head off for a hike in the woods, and you might come across beavers building a lodge, or flying squirrels gliding from tree to tree.

Study the scene below for 1 minute. Then cover the picture and answer the questions at the bottom of the page. Don't be tempted to peek at the questions first!

1. How many ducks are swimming on the lake?..............................

2. What is the color of the squirrel in the tree?..............................

3. How many fawns does the white-tailed deer have?..............................

4. What is the color of the woodpecker's head crest?..............................

EVERGLADES WORD HUNT

The marshes and rivers of the Everglades, in Florida, are home to many rare and wonderful animals, from wood storks, marsh rabbits, and American crocodiles, to the elusive Florida panther.

How many smaller words can you make from the letters in **EVERGLADES NATIONAL PARK?** All words must be 3 or more letters. Write your words below.

KEEPING SCORE:

- 3-letter words = 1 point
- 4-letter words = 2 points
- 5-letter words = 3 points
- Words with 6 or more letters = 5 points
- Score double points for any animal names!

HOW DID YOU DO?

Up to 15 points: Good effort
16–29 points: Excellent
30+ points: Outstanding!

DEADLY CRITTER CROSSWORD

SOLVE THE CROSSWORD CLUES TO REVEAL SOME OF THE MOST DANGEROUS ANIMALS IN THE UNITED STATES. YOU CAN USE THE WORD BANK AT THE BOTTOM OF THE PAGE TO HELP YOU, BUT BE AWARE, ONLY SOME OF THE ANIMALS IN THE WORD BANK ARE THE CORRECT ANSWERS!

CLUES:

ACROSS

1. Poisonous snake, famous for the noise it makes when it shakes its tail (11)

4. Wild canine that hunts in a pack (4)

7. Huge, scaly reptile with powerful jaws (9)

8. The black widow, brown recluse, and hobo are all types of which animal? (6)

CLUES:

DOWN

2. Eight-legged animal with a venomous sting at the end of its long, curved tail (8)

3. Ocean predator with several rows of razor-sharp teeth (5)

5. Big cat, also known as a mountain lion (6)

6. Large, powerful animal that is covered in fur and can be brown or black (4)

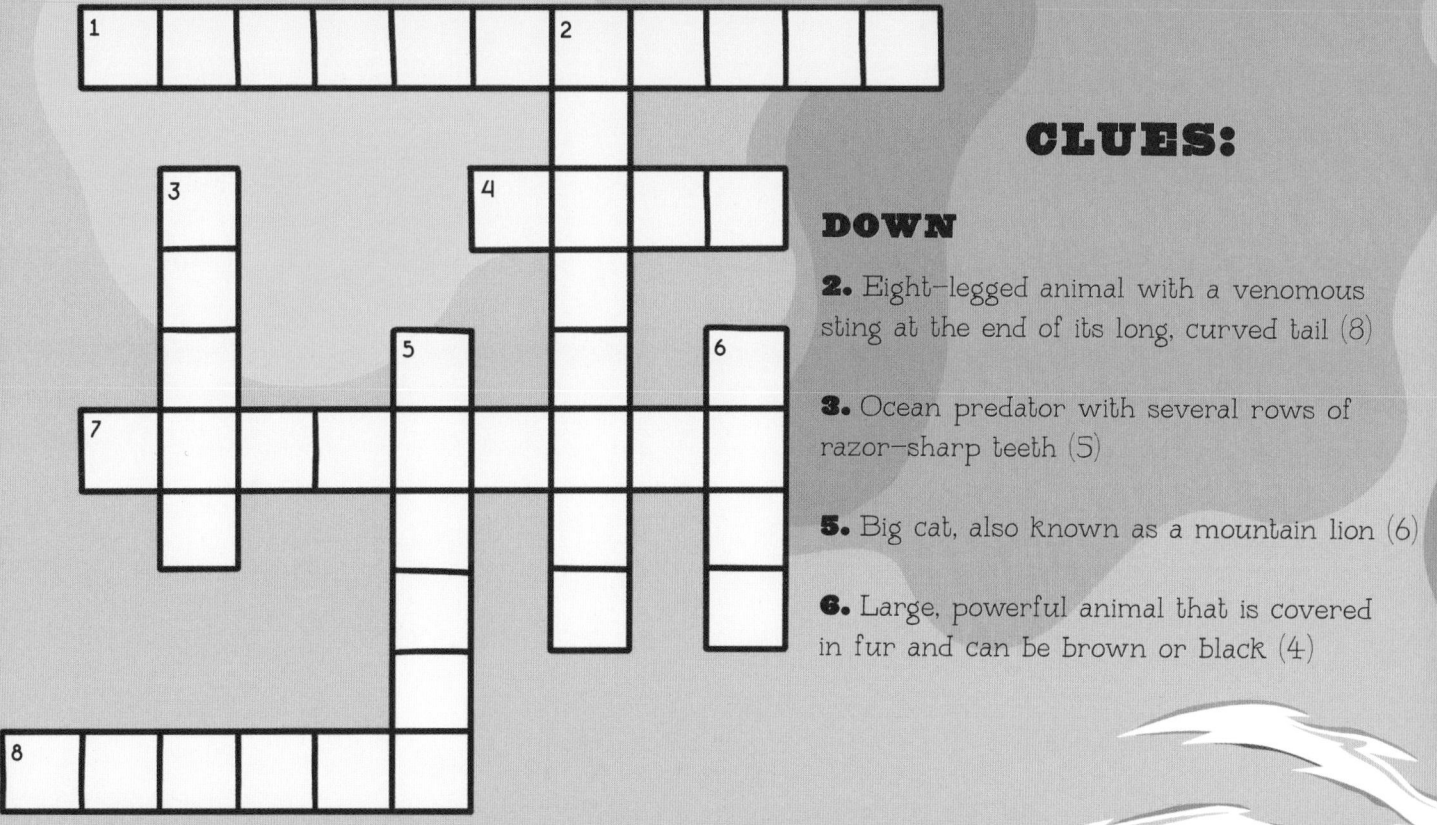

WORD BANK:

WHALE   COTTONMOUTH   ALLIGATOR   LYNX   BEAR   SCORPION   COUGAR   COYOTE
WOLF   SHARK   CROCODILE   OTTER   RATTLESNAKE   ORCA   SPIDER   GOPHER SNAKE

RANCH ROUNDUP

There are lots of ranches in the United States. Most raise cattle or sheep, but some raise bison, emus, or alpacas. Ranchers often ride horses to get around the ranch. Yee-haw!

Take a look at the busy cattle ranch scene. How many of the following animals can you spot? Write down your answers in the spaces.

BLACK-AND-WHITE CATTLE

BALD EAGLES

CATTLE WITH HORNS

DOGS

BLACK HORSES

Hold the Front Page!

Poncho Via, a Texas longhorn steer (male cow) from Alabama, hit the headlines in 2019 when his humongous horns set a new Guinness World Record. The distance between his horns, from tip to tip, measured over 10 feet and 7 inches—about as long as two adults reaching fingertip to fingertip!

Write a front-page story telling readers all about Poncho. Make sure the headline is snappy and attention-grabbing.

Daily Horn News

SPLIT THE WOLF PACKS

Gray wolves once roamed across two-thirds of the United States, but today, they are found in only a few states. The wolves live together in packs, and they will fight other packs if they stray onto their land!

Your task in this puzzle is to divide up a forest into four equal parts, so that it can be shared by four wolf packs. Each piece of forest must be identical in size and shape, and there must not be any land left over.

In this example, the forest can be split up into four parts of exactly the same size (four squares) and shape:

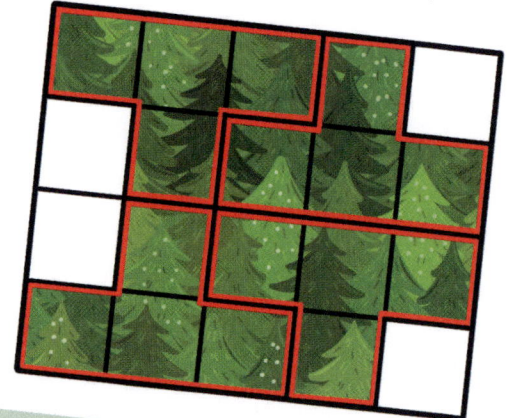

Use the example above to guide you, then tackle this puzzle.

HINT: First count up the total number of squares and divide by four. This will tell you how many squares each of your four pieces will need to be.

Draw a HUMMINGBIRD

Have you ever seen a hummingbird? These beautiful birds only live in North and South America, so most of the world doesn't get the chance to admire them. Follow these simple steps to draw a hummingbird in the space below, then color it in.

1. Draw the head and a long, thin beak.

2. Add an oval-shaped body.

3. Draw the wings and tail.

4. Add the tiny feet and eye, and color it in.

Hummingbirds get their name from the humming noise made by their wings flapping very fast—up to 200 times per second!

49

TRUE OR FALSE?

Read these animal-related statements about five states, and decide if each one is true or false. Circle your answers, then turn to page 63 to see if you were right.

1. The Kentucky Derby is a famous goat-racing event that takes place every May.

TRUE   FALSE

2. There are seven times more pigs than people in Iowa.

TRUE   FALSE

3. Maryland has a state crustacean, the blue crab.

TRUE   FALSE

4. The Maine Coon is the state cat for Maine.

TRUE   FALSE

5. Utah is famous for its lobsters—there are more lobsters caught in this state than in any other.

TRUE   FALSE

Hawaii Word Search

Many rare and beautiful animals live on the tropical islands of Hawaii. Can you find all nine Hawaiian animals in this word search? Circle them as you find them. Names may be up, down, or diagonal.

DOLPHIN

HOARY BAT

MONGOOSE

MONK SEAL

HUMPBACK WHALE

NENE

PUEO

GREEN SEA TURTLE

MANTA RAY

Deer States

Most US states have an official state mammal, and some states choose the same one. Fill in the missing letters below to uncover the names of the 10 states that all chose the white-tailed deer as their official mammal.

HINT: The missing letters are all vowels: a, e, i, o, u.

1. P_nnsylv_n__
2. S__th   C_r_l_n_
3. _h__
4. _ll_n__s
5. N_w   H_mpsh_r_
6. M_ss_ss_pp_
7. _rk_ns_s
8. N_br_sk_
9. G__rg__
10. M_ch_g_n

If you were in charge of choosing the official animals for your state, what would they be?

Land mammal: _____

Marine (ocean) mammal: _____

Bird: _____

Reptile: _____

WHO, WHAT, WHERE?

CAN YOU USE YOUR POWERS OF LOGIC TO WORK OUT WHICH NATIONAL PARK EACH OF THESE THREE CHILDREN VISITED AND WHICH ANIMAL THEY SAW THERE?

READ THE CLUES AND FILL IN THE GRID. ADD A CHECK MARK IF YOU KNOW SOMETHING IS TRUE, AND AN X IF SOMETHING IS FALSE. ONE CLUE HAS BEEN SOLVED ALREADY.

	OLIVER	ANTHONY	MIA
THEODORE ROOSEVELT NATIONAL PARK, NORTH DAKOTA			
CARLSBAD CAVERNS NATIONAL PARK, NEW MEXICO			
VOYAGEURS NATIONAL PARK, MINNESOTA			
BAT	✗	✗	✓
OTTER			✗
BISON			✗

CLUES:

1. THE CHILD WHO SAW BATS WAS NOT A BOY.
2. MIA VISITED CARLSBAD CAVERNS NATIONAL PARK.
3. THE CHILD WHO WENT TO VOYAGEURS NATIONAL PARK SAW AN ANIMAL THAT LIVES IN THE WATER.
4. OLIVER DID NOT SEE ANY BISON.

Copy the Mammoth

Some animal species that used to roam the US are extinct today, including woolly mammoths. These massive, elephant-like animals could once be found in Alaska. They had long, curved tusks and were covered in fur.

Draw a majestic woolly mammoth onto the empty grid. Use the top grid to help you: copy the picture square by square.

YOU CHOOSE

THERE ARE SO MANY AWESOME ANIMAL EXPERIENCES YOU CAN HAVE IN THE UNITED STATES. READ THE LIST BELOW, THEN NUMBER EACH EXPERIENCE IN THE ORDER YOU WOULD MOST LIKE TO DO THEM, FROM 1 (YOUR FAVORITE), ALL THE WAY DOWN TO 5 (YOUR LEAST FAVORITE). THEN FILL IN THE TICKET AT THE BOTTOM OF THE PAGE.

See the **BUFFALO ROUNDUP** at Custer State Park, South Dakota

GO DIVING WITH SHARKS IN RHODE ISLAND

WATCH BABY SEA TURTLES HATCH IN FLORIDA

GO WHALE WATCHING IN MASSACHUSETTS

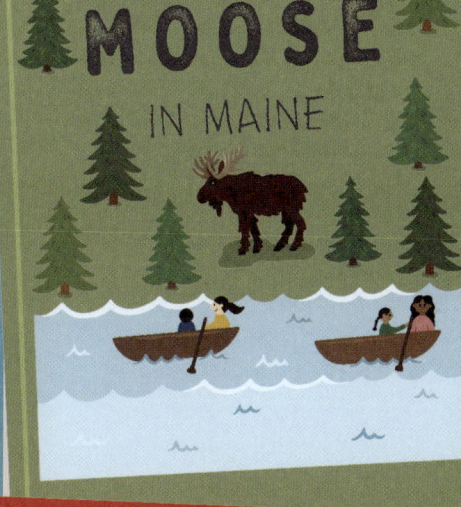

CANOE PAST MOOSE IN MAINE

TICKET

ADMITS: _____ (YOUR NAME)

AND _____ (NAME OF A FRIEND OR SOMEONE IN YOUR FAMILY)

TO _____ (NAME OF ACTIVITY)

I CHOSE THIS ACTIVITY BECAUSE:
_____
_____
_____
_____

ANSWERS

PAGE 7: WHERE AM I?
Tufted puffin: Alaska
Devils hole pupfish: Nevada
Nene: Hawaii
Island fox: California
Dall sheep: Alaska

PAGE 8: ALL-AMERICAN ANIMALS
The imposters are: panda, meerkat, and hippopotamus.

PAGE 9: NATIONAL PARK SCRAMBLE
Denali: Moose
Grand Teton: Bison
Great Smoky Mountains: Black Bear
Everglades: Alligator

PAGE 10: CLIMB THE MOUNTAIN

PAGE 12: BALANCE THE BISON
You need two moose to balance the scale.

PAGE 13: DESERT I-SPY

PAGE 14: WHERE'S MY MOM?

PAGE 15: ANIMALVILLE, USA
Hippopotamus, Florida, is the fake place.

PAGE 16: FOLLOW THE FLYWAY
Route C is the correct route.

PAGE 18: TAKE THE TRAIL

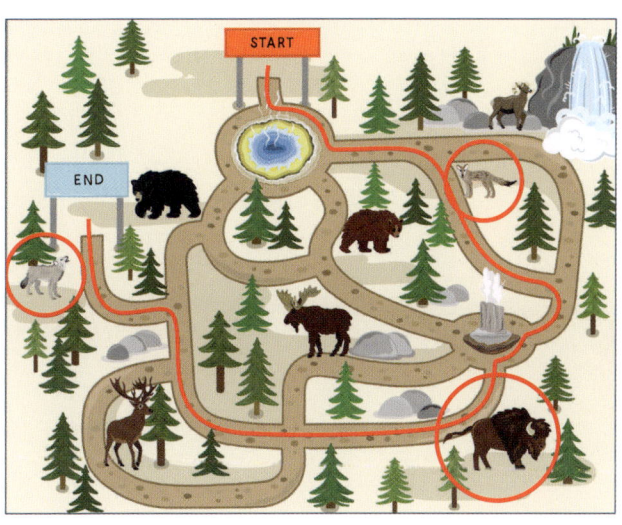

PAGE 19: QUIZ TIME!
1. b) Grizzly bear
2. c) Kangaroo rat
3. a) Pees on her
4. b) Blood

PAGE 20: ALL AT SEA

PAGE 21: BACKYARD BANDIT
1. A banana peel
2. A sock
3. A pair of glasses
4. A watermelon rind
5. An apple core
6. A toothbrush
7. An eggshell
8. A fish bone

PAGE 22: PRAIRIE DOG MAZE

PAGE 25: HIBERNATION CRISSCROSS

PAGE 26: ODD BIRD OUT

PAGE 27: SPIDER SEARCH
1. Black
2. Widow

The most venomous spider in the US is the black widow.

PAGE 28: WHAT'S ODD IN ALASKA?

PAGE 30: THE GREAT ARMADILLO COUNT

PAGE 32: SNAKE COLOR BY NUMBERS

PAGE 33: METAMORPHOSIS MAZE

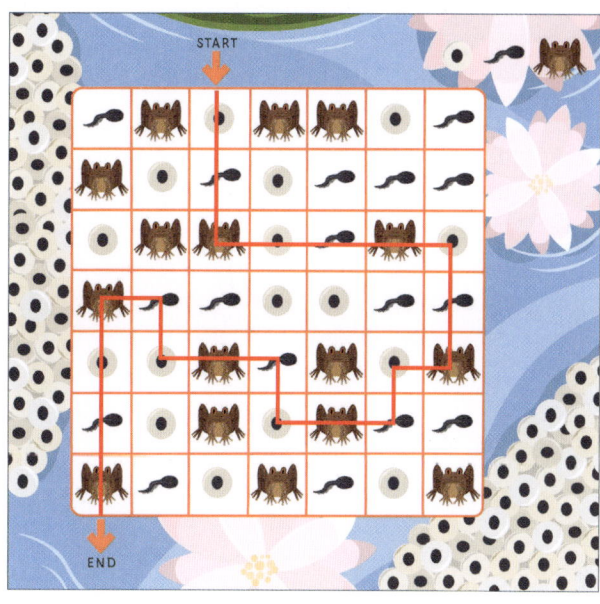

PAGE 34: FAR-OUT FESTIVALS
The two fake festivals are the Croc Jump Festival and Hank's Hound Hoedown.

PAGE 35: COUNT THE CATCH
There are nine fish left to catch.
Bear 1 catches six fish (twice as many as Bear 2).
Bear 2 catches three fish.

PAGE 37: MINIBEAST SUDOKU

PAGE 38: UNDER THE SEA

PAGE 40: CRACK THE CODES
Fastest: Pronghorn.
Pronghorns can run at 60 miles per hour.
Biggest: Bison.
Tallest: Moose.

PAGE 41: HIDE-AND-SEEK

PAGE 42: NICKNAME THAT STATE
Wisconsin: Badger State
Louisiana: Pelican State
Michigan: Wolverine State
Oregon: Beaver State

PAGE 43: STUDY THE SCENE
1. Three
2. Red
3. Two
4. Red

PAGE 45: DEADLY CRITTER CROSSWORD

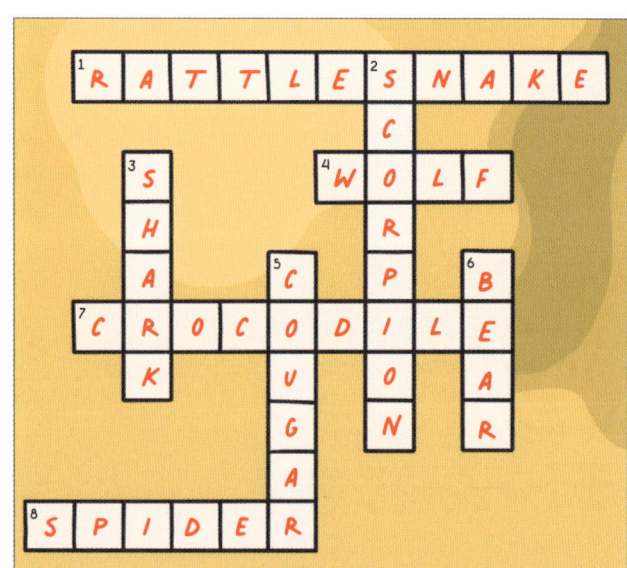

PAGE 46: RANCH ROUNDUP

Black-and-white cattle: four
Cattle with horns: three
Black horses: one
Bald eagles: two
Dogs: three

PAGE 48: SPLIT THE WOLF PACKS

PAGE 50: TRUE OR FALSE?

1. False. The Kentucky Derby is a famous racing event for horses, not goats.
2. True.
3. True.
4. True.
5. False. Utah is landlocked and doesn't have any coastline.

PAGE 51: HAWAII WORD SEARCH

PAGE 52: DEER STATES

1. Pennsylvania
2. South Carolina
3. Ohio
4. Illinois
5. New Hampshire
6. Mississippi
7. Arkansas
8. Nebraska
9. Georgia
10. Michigan

PAGE 54: WHO, WHAT, WHERE?

PAGE 55: FIND THE FISH

The missing piece is number 3.

First American Edition 2022
Kane Miller, A Division of EDC Publishing

Animals of the USA Activity Book © 2022 Quarto Publishing plc

Published by arrangement with Ivy Kids, an imprint of The Quarto Group.
All rights reserved. No part of this book may be reproduced, transmitted,
or stored in an information retrieval system in any form or by any means, graphic,
electronic, or mechanical, including photocopying, taping, and recording,
without prior written permission from the publisher.

For information contact:
Kane Miller, A Division of EDC Publishing
5402 S 122nd E Ave
Tulsa, OK 74146
www.kanemiller.com
www.myubam.com

Manufactured in Guangdong, China TT1021

ISBN: 978-1-68464-285-4

1 2 3 4 5 6 7 8 9 10